MENOTTI

ARIAS FOR SOPRANO

10 ARIAS FROM 7 OPERAS

T0081840

The recording is a collaboration of Hal Leonard and G. Schirmer, Cincinnati Opera, The College-Conservatory of Music, Cincinnati, and WGUC, Cincinnati, with support from the J. Ralph and Patricia Corbett Foundation.

Evans Mirageas, producer

ED 4384
ISBN 978-1-4234-2751-3

G. SCHIRMER, *Inc.*

DISTRIBUTED BY

HAL•LEONARD®
CORPORATION

7777 W. BLUEMOUND RD. P.O. BOX 13819 MILWAUKEE, WI 53213

www.schirmer.com
www.halleonard.com

GIAN CARLO MENOTTI
(1911–2007)

Gian Carlo Menotti was born on July 7, 1911, in Cadegliano, Italy. At the age of 7, under the guidance of his mother, he began to compose songs, and four years later he wrote the words and music of his first opera, *The Death of Pierrot*. In 1923 he began his formal musical training at the Verdi Conservatory in Milan. Following the death of his father, his mother took him to the United States, where he was enrolled at Philadelphia's Curtis Institute of Music. There he completed his musical studies, working in composition under Rosario Scalero.

His first mature work, the one-act opera buffa, *Amelia al Ballo*, was premiered in 1937, a success that led to a commission from the National Broadcasting Company to write an opera especially for radio, *The Old Maid and the Thief*, the first such commission ever given. His first ballet, *Sebastian*, followed in 1944, and for this he wrote the scenario as well as the score. After the premiere of his Piano Concerto in 1945, Menotti returned to opera with *The Medium*, shortly joined by *The Telephone*, both enjoying international success.

The Consul, Menotti's first full-length work, won the Pulitzer Prize and the New York Drama Critics Circle award as the best musical play of the year in 1954. By far Menotti's best-known work is the Christmas classic *Amahl and the Night Visitors*, composed for NBC-TV in 1951. This beloved opera celebrated the 50th anniversary of its premiere in 2001, and continues to receive hundreds of performances annually.

Menotti wrote the text to all his operas, the original language being English in every case, with the exception of *Amelia al Ballo*, *The Island God*, and *The Last Savage*, which were first set to Italian words. Recent operas include *The Singing Child* (1993) and *Goya* (1986), written for Plácido Domingo and given its premiere by The Washington Opera. In the summer of 2004 Domingo reprised the role at Vienna's Theater an der Wien. Menotti's most recent vocal works are *Jacob's Prayer* (1997), a commission from the American Choral Directors Association, *Gloria*, written as part of a composite Mass celebrating the 1995 Nobel Peace Prize, *For the Death of Orpheus*, with a premiere by the Atlanta Symphony Orchestra led by Robert Shaw in November 1990, and *Llama de Amor Viva*, premiered in April 1991. A trio for the Verdehr Trio received its world premiere at the Spoleto Festival on Menotti's 85th birthday in July 1996.

In addition to the numerous operatic works, Menotti has enriched the artistic world with ballets, including *Errand into the Maze* (in the repertory of the Martha Graham Dance Company), and *The Unicorn, the Gorgon, and the Manticore*; *Pastorale for Piano and Strings* (1934); *Poemetti*, a suite of piano pieces for children (1937); *The Hero* (1952), a song on a text by Robert Horan; and *Canti della Lontananza*, a cycle of seven songs (1967). He also wrote the librettos to Samuel Barber's operas *Vanessa* and *A Hand of Bridge*.

1958 saw the opening of Menotti's own festival, the Festival of Two Worlds, in Spoleto, Italy. Devoted to the cultural collaboration of Europe and America in a program embracing all the arts, the Spoleto Festival has gone on to be one of the most popular festivals in Europe. The festival literally became "of two worlds" in 1977 with the founding of Spoleto USA in Charleston, South Carolina, which he led until 1993 when he became Director of the Rome Opera. Well into his 90s he continued to direct opera at Spoleto and elsewhere. During the 2005-06 season *The Consul* was produced at Teatro Regio in Italy; performances in the 2004-05 season included productions at the Arizona Opera and in Zurich, Switzerland. Menotti died in Monaco on February 1, 2007, at age 95.

In 1984 Menotti was awarded the Kennedy Center Honor for lifetime achievement in the arts. He was chosen the 1991 "Musician of the Year" by Musical America, inaugurating worldwide tributes to the composer in honor of his 80th birthday. His music has been published by G. Schirmer since 1946.

CONTENTS

Singers on the CD:
Sonia Rodríguez Bermejo (tracks 3, 4)
Carol Dusdieker (tracks 2, 6)
Tanya Kruse (track 8)
Audrey Luna (track 10)
Helen Lyons (track 9)
Danielle Walker (tracks 1, 5, 7)

Pianists:
Mark Gibson (track 6)
Marcus Küchle (tracks 9, 10)
Matthew Lobaugh (tracks 1, 3, 4, 5, 7)
Carol Walker (track 2)
Richard Walters (track 8)

NOTES ON THE ARIAS

AMELIA AL BALLO
• music and libretto by Gian Carlo Menotti
• first performed on April 1, 1937 at the Academy of Music in Philadelphia

Vola intanto l'ora insonne

in one act
setting: Milan, Amelia's apartment
character: Amelia

Amelia is dressed to go to a ball when her husband bursts in, demanding to know the identity of Amelia's secret lover. She eventually relents (after her husband promises to take her to the ball) and reveals that it is the man who lives upstairs. The husband rushes off to kill him. Amelia, now alone, bemoans her fate, resigned to missing the grandest ball of the year.

THE OLD MAID AND THE THIEF
• music and libretto by Gian Carlo Menotti
• commissioned by NBC Radio; first performed in a live broadcast on April 22, 1939

Steal me, sweet thief

in one act, from scene 6
setting: a small town somewhere in the United States, the present; the kitchen of Miss Todd's house
character: Laetitia

Miss Todd, an aging old maid desperate for male company, takes in a beggar who turns out to be a thief. She won't let him leave, going so far as to steal liquor (to avoid the shame of being seen buying it) to keep him happy. Alone in the kitchen, the unmarried Laetitia, Miss Todd's maid, romantically daydreams about Bob the beggar while mending and pressing his trousers.

THE MEDIUM
• music and libretto by Gian Carlo Menotti
• first performed on May 8, 1946 at Columbia University, New York City; opened on Broadway (on a double bill with *The Telephone*) on May 1, 1947 at the Ethel Barrymore Theatre, New York City

The Black Swan

from Act I
setting: the outskirts of a great city, the present; Madame Flora's parlor
character: Monica

As she holds a séance for several customers, Baba (Madame Flora), a phony medium, feels a hand at her throat. Blaming the mute boy Toby, she beats him to confess that he was actually the one who touched her. Monica, Baba's teenage daughter, pulls her terrified and deranged mother away from Toby, rests Baba's head on her lap, and sings to calm her.

Monica's Waltz

from Act II
setting: the outskirts of a great city, the present; Madame Flora's parlor
character: Monica

The mute Toby has just performed a puppet show for Monica, which she has applauded. As she sings this aria, Toby, in love with her, dances about the stage, barefooted.

Most of the material in this section was previously published in the *G. Schirmer American Aria Anthology*, edited by Richard Walters.

THE TELEPHONE
or L'amour à trois
• music and libretto by Gian Carlo Menotti
• first performed on February 18, 1947 at the Heckscher Theater, New York City; opened on Broadway
  (on a double bill with *The Medium*) on May 1, 1947 at the Ethel Barrymore Theatre

Hello! Oh, Margaret, it's you

in one act
setting: the present; Lucy's apartment
character: Lucy

This short, comic opera looks at the frustrations of love in the age of the telephone. Ben has arrived at Lucy's apartment to tell her he is leaving town for a while that very day. As he is attempting to propose to her, Lucy's phone rings. She answers and begins a chatty conversation with Margaret, to Ben's great frustration.

THE CONSUL
• music and libretto by Gian Carlo Menotti
• first performed on March 1, 1950 at the Schubert Theater in Philadelphia; opened on Broadway on
  March 15, 1950 at the Ethel Barrymore Theatre, New York City

The Foreign Woman's Aria

from Act I, scene 2
setting: a European police state, the present; the Consulate of a neighboring country
character: the Foreign Woman

A group of desperate citizens waits day after day to see the Consul of a neighboring (free) country (who never appears in the opera), pleading with his secretary to obtain exit visas. An Italian immigrant, called the Foreign Woman, introduces herself to the secretary by saying, "Scusi, Signorina, ma io non capisco." Mr. Kofner, who also seeks a visa, offers to help by translating for her as she tells her story. (Mr. Kofner's lines have been eliminated for this solo aria edition.)

Mio Signor, io vengo per mia figlia,	*Sir, I come because of my daughter,*
l'unica mia creatura.	*my only baby.*
Fuggì da casa con un dei vostri soldati	*She fled from home with one of your soldiers*
quando era ancora una bambina.	*when she was still a child.*
Per tre anni non ebbi sue notizie;	*For three years I've had no news from her;*
la cercai dappertutto.	*I have searched for her everywhere.*
Avevo ormai perduta ogni speranza	*I had lost every hope, up to now,*
di rivedere la mia Giulia,	*of seeing my Giulia again,*
ma stamani la lettera è arrivata,	*but this morning the letter arrived,*
e così mi scrive la mia povera bambina.	*and my poor child writes as follows:*
"Mammina, mi sono ammalata	*"Mamma dear, I am ill*
e temo di morire.	*and I am afraid I will die.*
Mio marito m'abbandonata	*My husband abandoned me*
con un piccino di tre mesi	*with a little three-month old child*
in questo paese straniero.	*in this foreign country.*
Mamma, vieni!	*Mamma, come!*
Ho tanto bisogno del tuo aiuto."	*I need your help so much."*
È proprio così che mi scrive la mia povera bambina.	*That is exactly what my poor child wrote to me.*
Immagini la mia pena.	*You can imagine my suffering.*
Io voglio andar vicino a la mia Giulia	*I want to go to Giulia's side*
e prendere cura del piccino.	*and take care of the little one.*

Translation by Martha Gerhart

To this we've come

from Act II, scene 2
setting: a European police state, the present; the Consulate of a neighboring country
character: Magda Sorel

Magda's baby son has died, and her mother-in-law is dying. Her freedom activist husband has fled to the nation represented by the Consul, waiting for Magda to join him. She has been fruitlessly trying to get an exit visa. Magda, hounded constantly by the secret police, finally gets her chance to speak with the secretary at the consulate, but, as has happened before, is put off again, asked to fill out endless and useless bureaucratic forms and to bring documents impossible to attain. She loses her temper in frustration and is warned that she will be asked to leave if her angry behavior continues. Magda collects herself and responds with great humanity.

THE SAINT OF BLEECKER STREET
• music and libretto by Gian Carlo Menotti
• opened on Broadway on December 27, 1954 at the Broadway Theatre, New York City

Oh, Sweet Jesus

from Act I, scene 1
setting: Greenwich Village, New York City, the present; a cold-water flat on Bleecker Street
character: Annina

Michele and Annina, brother and sister, are both driven by Catholicism, she by her deep faith and the stigmata that appear on her hands, he by hatred of religion. In this aria Annina is in the throes of a vision and the painful appearance of stigmata, surrounded by awed onlookers.

Be good to her

from Act II
setting: Greenwich Village, New York City, the present; a wedding celebration at an Italian restaurant
character: Annina

Salvatore is impatient with his bride Carmela as she giggles. Carmela's friend Annina tells Salvatore to be gentle with his new wife, whom she loves very much.

THE LABYRINTH
• music and libretto by Gian Carlo Menotti
• commissioned by NBC television, first broadcast on March 3, 1963

The Bride's Song

in one act
setting: allegorical
character: the Bride

The Labyrinth was conceived for television, with a musical/dramatic design that exploited the possibilities of that medium. A bride and groom, on their honeymoon at a hotel, cannot find the key to their room, and become separated and lost.

MENOTTI

ARIAS FOR SOPRANO

Vola intanto l'ora insonne
(While I waste these precious hours)
from AMELIA AL BALLO

Gian Carlo Menotti

Steal me, sweet thief
from
THE OLD MAID AND THE THIEF

Gian Carlo Menotti

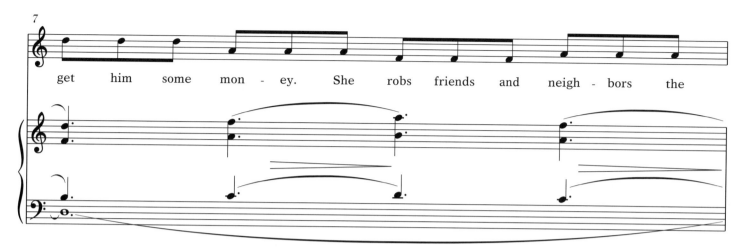

get him some mon-ey. She robs friends and neigh-bors the

Tempo I

club and the church. He takes all the mon-ey with a

smile that en-tran-ces... but still makes no ad-vanc - es. The

old wo-man sighs and makes lan-guid eyes.

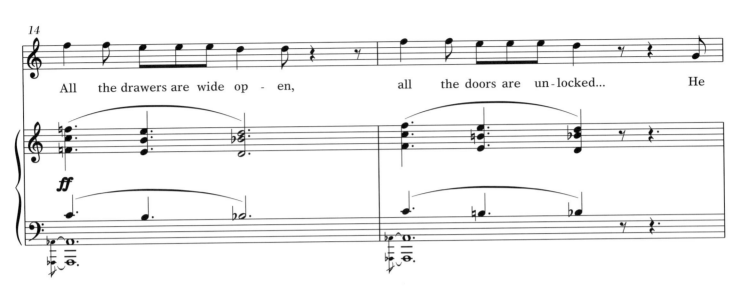

All the drawers are wide op - en, all the doors are un-locked... He

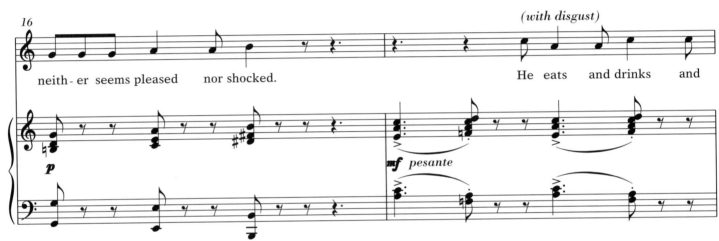

neith- er seems pleased nor shocked. *(with disgust)* He eats and drinks and

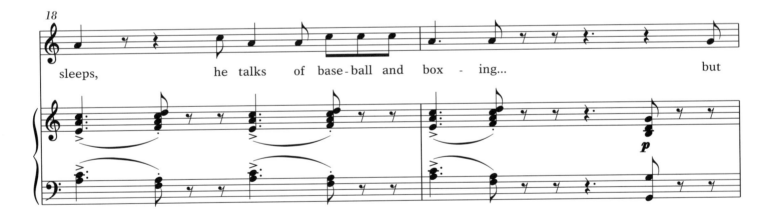

sleeps, he talks of base-ball and box - ing... but

that is all. What ___ a curse for a wo - man is a tim-id man!

Steal my breath _____ be - fore it will fade. Steal my lips, steal my heart,

steal my cheeks, steal, oh steal my breath _____ and make me die be -

fore _____ death _____ will steal her prey. Oh, steal me!

For time's flight is steal - ing my youth. _____

The Black Swan
from
THE MEDIUM

Gian Carlo Menotti

bri - dal gown, And my lamp is lost, and my lamp is lost.

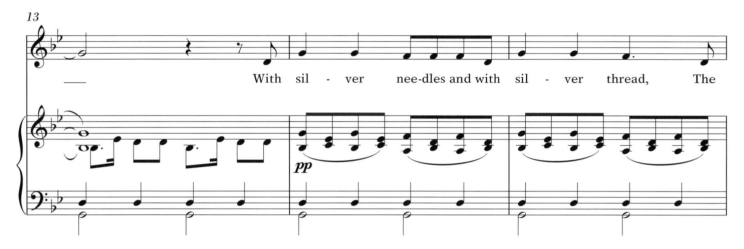

With sil - ver nee-dles and with sil - ver thread, The

stars stitch a shroud for the dy - ing sun. O black swan,

where, oh, where has my lov - er gone? I had giv - en him a

kiss of fire, And a gold-en ring, and a gold-en ring.

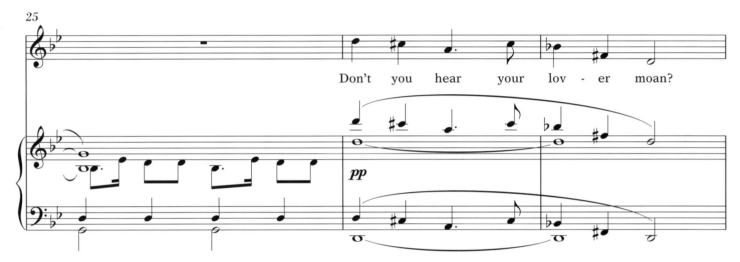

Don't you hear your lov-er moan?

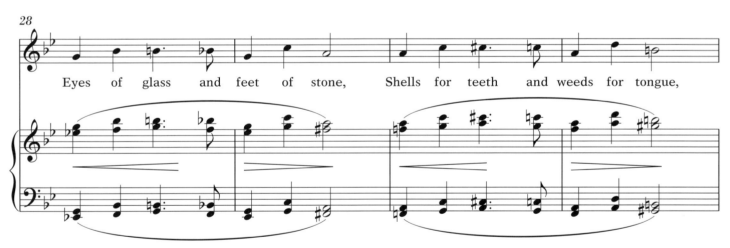

Eyes of glass and feet of stone, Shells for teeth and weeds for tongue,

Deep, deep, down in the riv-er's bed he's look-ing for the ring.

Eyes wide o-pen, nev-er a-sleep, he's look-ing for the ring,

look-ing for the ring. The spools un-rav-el and the nee-dles break. The

sun is bur-ied and the stars weep. O black wave,

O black wave,___ take me a-way with you. I will share with you my

gold - en hair, and my bri - dal crown, and my bri - dal crown.

Oh, ___ take me down with you. Take me down to my wan - d'ring

lov - er with my child un - born, with my child un - born. ___

Monica's Waltz
from
THE MEDIUM

Gian Carlo Menotti

*(Monica is sitting in front of the puppet theater watching a performance)

(The puppets have fallen in a heap.
Toby comes out to acknowledge
Monica's applause.)

MONICA:
(liberamente)

Bra - vo! And af -ter the the -a -ter, sup-per and dance. Mu-sic! Um -pa - pa, um -pa - pa,

*Menotti's stage directions are retained for the singer's benefit. They are not, however, to be employed in a
  concert presentation of the aria.

Up in the sky some-one is play-ing a trom-bone and a gui-tar.

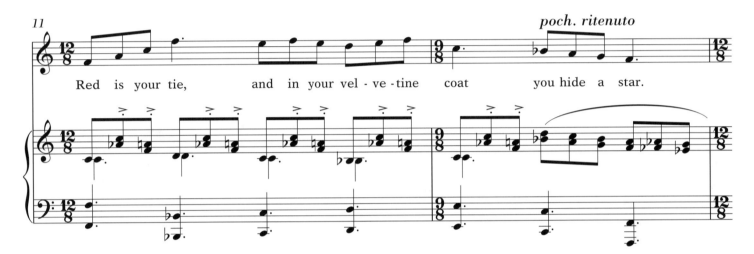

Red is your tie, and in your vel-ve-tine coat you hide a star.

poch. ritenuto

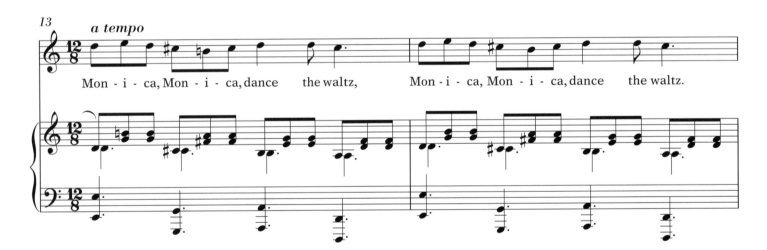

a tempo

Mon-i-ca, Mon-i-ca, dance the waltz, Mon-i-ca, Mon-i-ca, dance the waltz.

Fol-low me, moon and sun, keep time with me, one two three one.

If you're not shy, pin up my hair with your star, and buck-le my shoe.

poco rit.

And when you fly, please hold on tight to my waist, I'm fly-ing with you. O,

a tempo

Mon - i - ca, Mon - i - ca, dance the waltz, Mon - i - ca, Mon - i - ca, dance the waltz.

Fol-low me, moon and sun, Fol-low me, fol-low, fol - low

me, fol-low me, fol-low, fol - low me.

(Toby seizes Monica abruptly by the arm. She turns and looks at him in complete astonishment.)

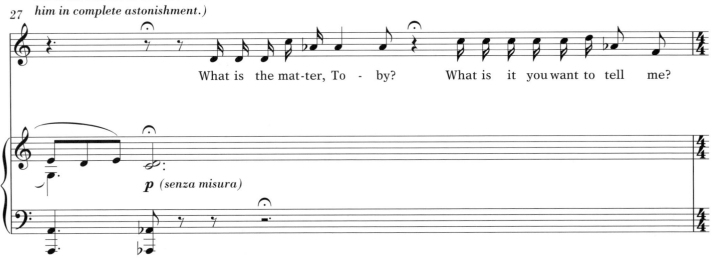

What is the mat-ter, To - by? What is it you want to tell me?

p (senza misura)

*(He looks at her in desperation,
and gently touches her face)*

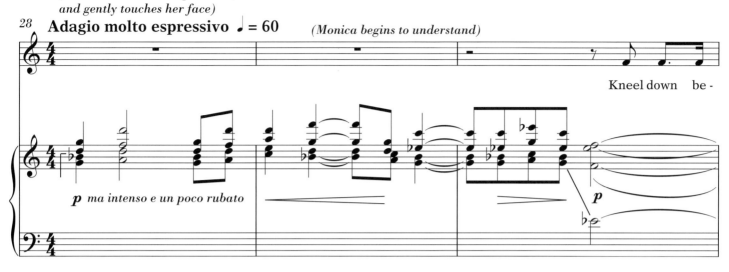

(Monica begins to understand)

Kneel down be-

(Toby kneels)

*(She kneels behind Toby, as if the words were coming from him,
and makes Toby look up as if she were standing in front of him)*

fore me, and now, tell me...

Mon - i - ca, Mon - i - ca, can't you see,___ that my heart is bleed-ing, bleed-ing for you?

I loved you, Mon - i - ca, all my life,___ with all my breath, with all my blood.

You haunt the mir-ror of my sleep, you are my night. You ___ are my light and the

jail-er of my day.___ *(Quickly she gets up and stands before him)* How dare you, scoun-drel, talk to me like that! Don't you know who I

am? I'm the Queen of A - roun-del! I shall have you put in

(She kneels behind him again. Toby, falling in with the game, mimics her words with gestures.)

chains! _____ You are my prin-cess, you are my queen, _

p dolce

poco rit.

and I'm on - ly To - by, one of your slaves, and still I love you and al - ways loved you

48

a tempo

poco animando

with all my breath, with all my blood. I love your laugh-ter, I love your hair,

50

I love your deep and noc-tur - nal eyes. I love your soft hands, so white and winged,

più f *cresc.*

52

rall.

(She stands up before him)

a tempo

I love the slen - der branch of your throat. To - by, don't speak to me like

f

pp subito

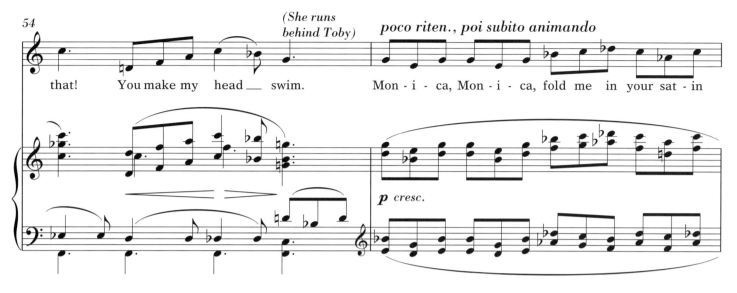

(She caresses his head. Then lifting his tear-stained face, looks into his eyes.)

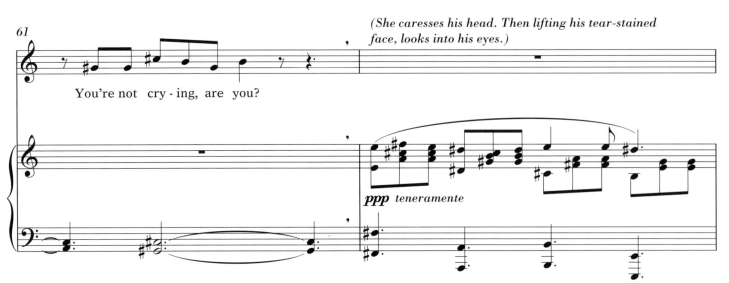

You're not cry-ing, are you?

To - by, I want you to know that you have _____

_____ the most beau-ti-ful voice _____ in _____ the world! _____

Hello! Oh, Margaret, it's you

from
THE TELEPHONE

Gian Carlo Menotti

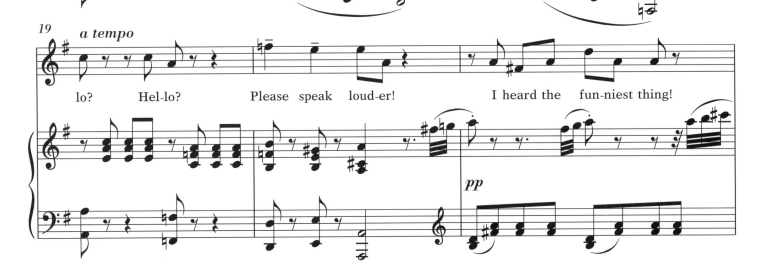

Jean? You must tell them that I send them my love. And how is

Ur - su - la, and how is Nat - a - lie, and how is Ro - sa - lie? I hope she's got - ten

o - ver her cold. And how is your moth - er, and how is your fa - ther,

and how is dear lit - tle gran - ny?

(nodding)

Allegro con brio

Ha!

f brillante

read-y told me that. No my dar - ling, of course I won't for-get!

Yes... yes... good-bye, my dear, good-bye... Yes, my dar - ling, good-

bye... Yes! Ha! ha! Ha!

ha! Ah!

The Foreign Woman's Aria

from

THE CONSUL

Gian Carlo Menotti

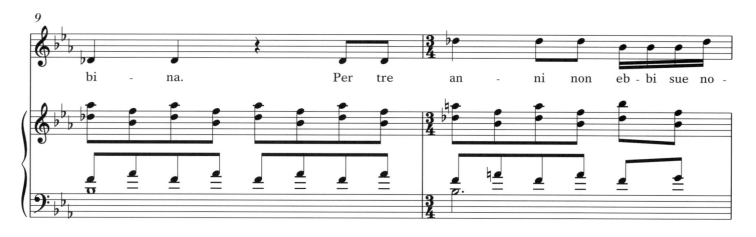

bi - na. Per tre an - ni non eb - bi sue no -

poco rit.

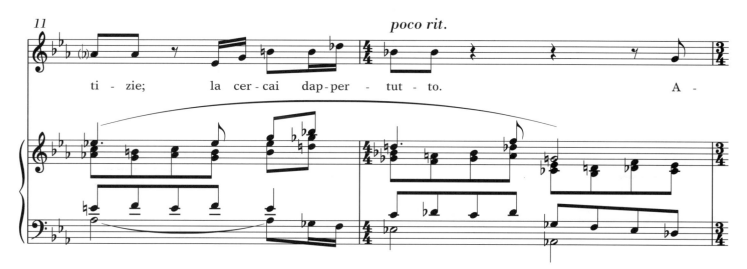

ti - zie; la cer - cai dap - per - tut - to. A -

a tempo

ve-vo or-mai per - du-ta o-gni spe-ran - za di ri - ve-de - re la mia

(She produces the precious letter from her bosom.)

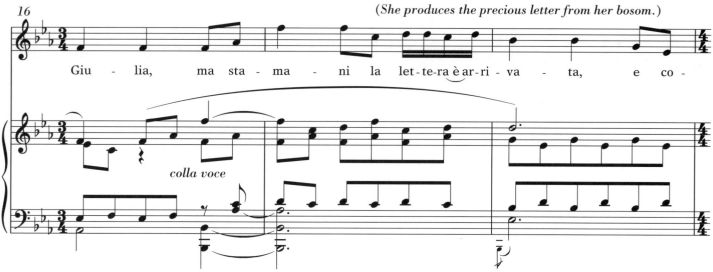

Giu - lia, ma sta-ma - ni la let-te-ra è ar-ri - va - ta, e co -

colla voce

(reading from the letter)

sì mi scri - ve la mia po - ve - ra bam - bi - na. "Mam -

più agitato

mi - na, mi so - no am - ma - la - ta e te - mo di mo - ri - re.

Mio ma - ri - to m'ab - ban - do - na - ta con un pic - ci - no di tre me - si in

cresc. poco a poco

que - sto pa - e - se stra - nie - ro. Mam - ma, vie - ni! Ho

f espr.

tan - to bi - so-gno del tuo a - iu - - to."

È pro - prio co - sì che mi scri - ve la mia po - ve - ra bam - bi - na. Im-

ma-gi-ni la mia pe - na. Io vo-glio an-dar vi - ci-no a la mia Giu - lia e

pren - de - re cu - ra del pic - ci - no.

To this we've come
from
THE CONSUL

Gian Carlo Menotti

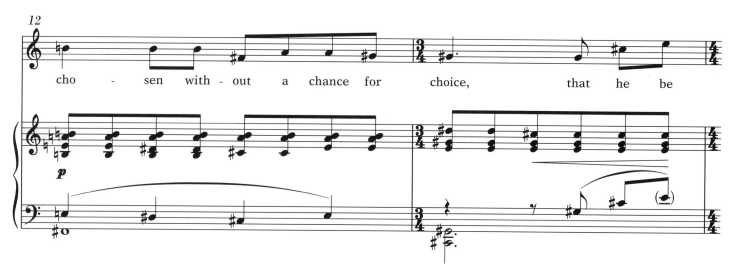

cho - sen with - out a chance for choice, that he be

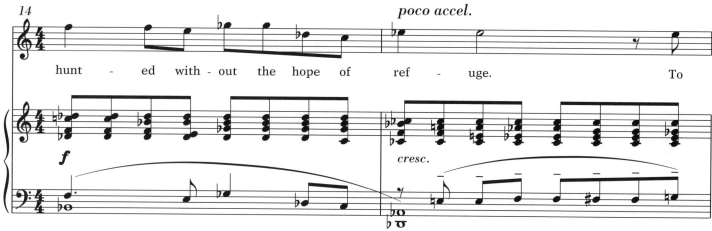

hunt - ed with - out the hope of ref - uge. To

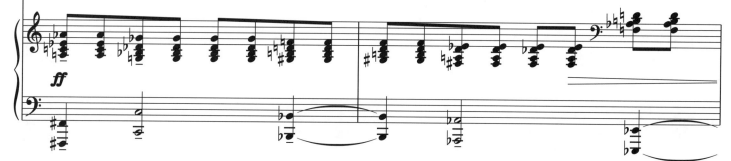

this we've come, to this we've come; ____ and you, you,

too, shall weep. If to men, not to God, we now must

heart can still be ex-plained? Is there one— an - y one who still may

care? Tell me, sec - re - ta - ry, tell me. Have

(Libermente)

you ev - er seen the Con - sul? Does he speak, does he breathe?

Have you ev - er spo-ken to him?

Allegro

What is your name? Mag-da Sor-el. Age? Thir-ty-three.

Col-or of eyes? Col-or of hair? Sin-gle or mar-ried? Re-

li-gion and race? Place of birth, Fa-ther's name, Moth-er's name?

(Tearing the paper she holds in her hand, Magda rushes to the desk, takes up a great stack of papers from there, and begins to hurl them about the room.)

Pa-pers! Pa-pers!

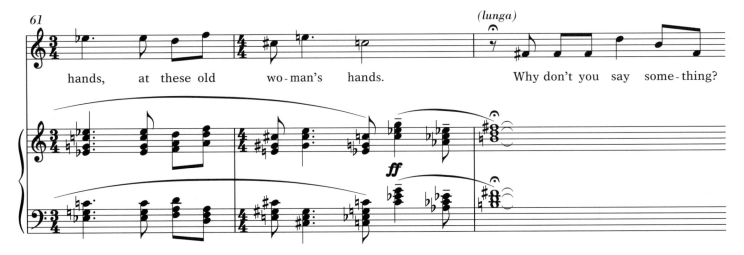

Are-n't you sec-re-ta-ries hu-man be-ings like us?

Allegro

(with mounting anguish)

What is your name? Mag-da Sor-el. Age? Thir-ty-three.

What will your pa-pers do? They can-not stop the clock. They are too

thin an ar-mor a-gainst a bul-let. What is your name? Mag-da Sor-el.

[breve]

Age? Thir - ty - three. _____ What does that mat-ter?

All that mat - ters is that the time is late, that I'm a - fraid and I

need your help. What is your name?

Meno mosso
(with great dignity and simplicity)

What is your name? What is your name? This is my an - swer: My name

is wo-man. Age: Still young. Col-or of hair:

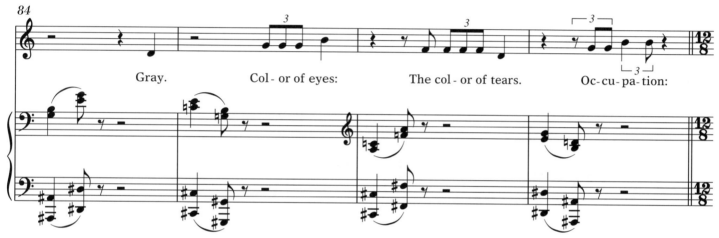

Gray. Col-or of eyes: The col-or of tears. Oc-cu-pa-tion:

Allegro agitato

Wait - ing. Wait - ing.

cresc., poco a poco

Wait - ing. wait - ing,

day ____ nei-ther ink nor seal ____ shall cage ____ our

souls, _____ That day will come, _____ that

day will come! _____

tutta forza

Oh, Sweet Jesus
from
THE SAINT OF BLEECKER STREET

Gian Carlo Menotti

gain with-stand _____ the trial?   Where am I?   Who are these peo- ple?

When have I seen this road be-fore, when   this bar-ren hill?   What is this drunk-en crowd wait-ing for? _

Ah, _____   dread-ful pre - sen - ti ment!

Lento e pesante

Ea-ger and loud, they push and sway un-der the fes - ti-val sun.

poco a poco accel. fine al Moderato e sostenuto

What do they want? What are they wait-ing for? I can-not see.

Eh! Don't push me. Let me see. Please make

Moderato e sostenuto

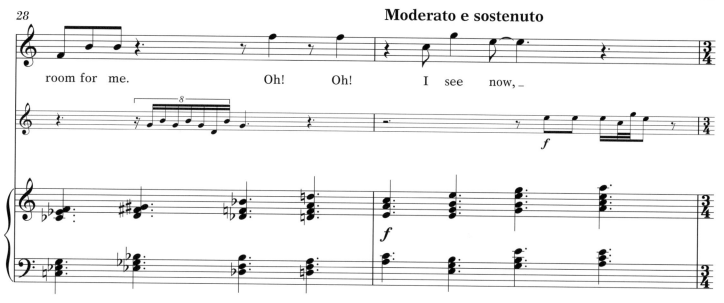

room for me. Oh! Oh! I see now, _

I see now! Oh, blind - ing sight!

Oh, pain! Oh, love! _____

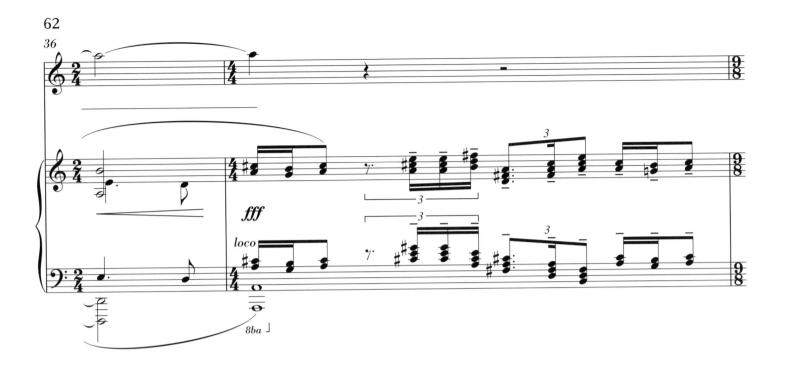

They come up the bend-ing road in

gold - en ar - mor, the sol - diers, and a-mong them a pur-ple cloak. My

Je - sus! How large a cross for one man to bear! Dust in His mouth and salt of bit-ter

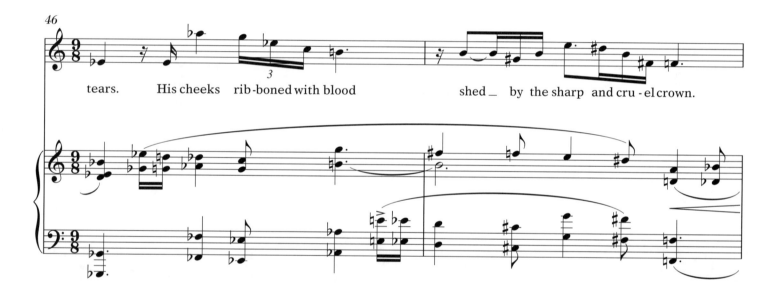

tears. His cheeks rib-boned with blood shed __ by the sharp and cru - el crown.

Ah! But His eyes! _____

Who ev - er saw in a man's eyes _____ such pa - tient love? _____

Ah! _____ He fal - ters. They are on Him with whips. He strug - gles on a - gain.

Some - one is weep - ing. Where? _

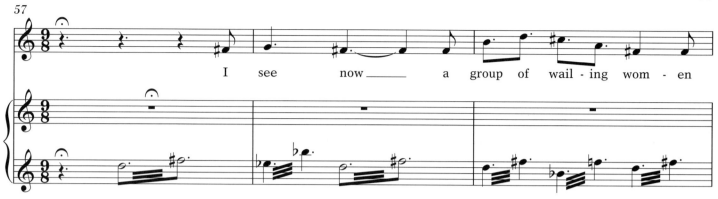

I see now ____ a group of wail - ing wom - en

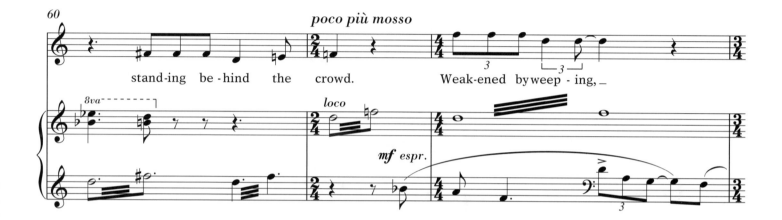

poco più mosso

stand-ing be - hind the crowd. Weak-ened by weep - ing, __

they sway like reeds as they slow - ly move. Tall a - mongst them, Her

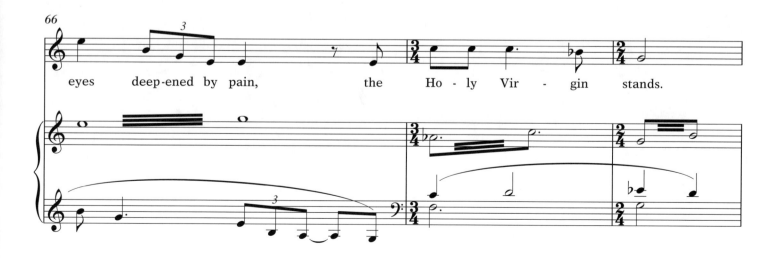

eyes deep-ened by pain, the Ho - ly Vir - gin stands.

Why, Mar - y, why did you come? No cross can weigh nor

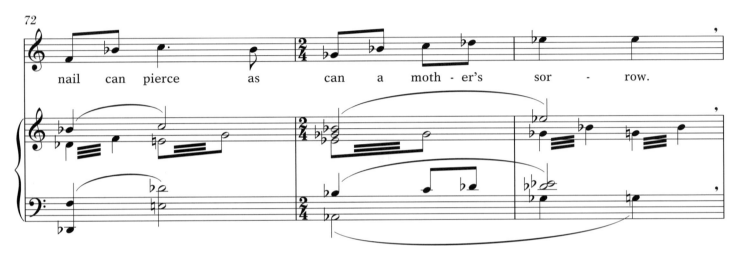

nail can pierce as can a moth-er's sor - row.

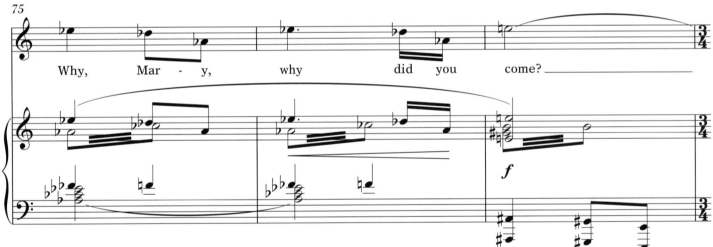

Why, Mar - y, why did you come? _____

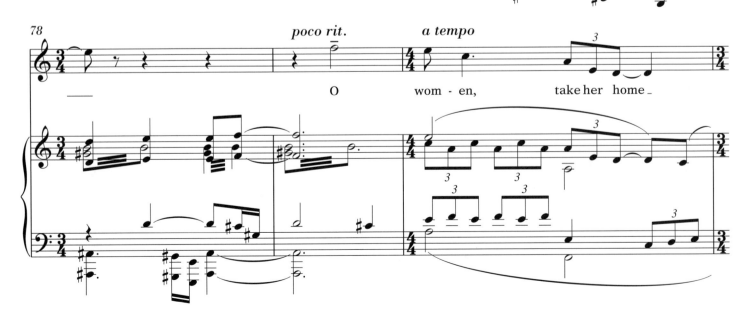

poco rit.   a tempo

O wom - en, take her home _

When our God will die, on-ly her Son will bear the ag - o - ny. Oh,

take her, take her home. It is her ver-y flesh that will be torn by spear and

nail. Oh, take her, take her home.

ly - ing there. _____ His

palm is now held o - pen. Those Hands that gave _ us

all, _____ by us _____ are _____ to be pierced.

Sol - dier, sol - dier, have mer - cy on

Him. For He a - lone is your

Sav - iour. The nail is held in place.

The huge ham - mer is raised._____ Ah_____

114 *pesantissimo ma poco più mosso*

Be good to her
from
THE SAINT OF BLEECKER STREET

Gian Carlo Menotti

dressed in white, a diff-erent bride with a bright, red

rose-bush in her heart and bright, black stars in her eyes.

She'll make you a good wife, Sal-va-to-re. You'll see. Be

good to her, be kind.

The Bride's Song
from
THE LABYRINTH

Gian Carlo Menotti

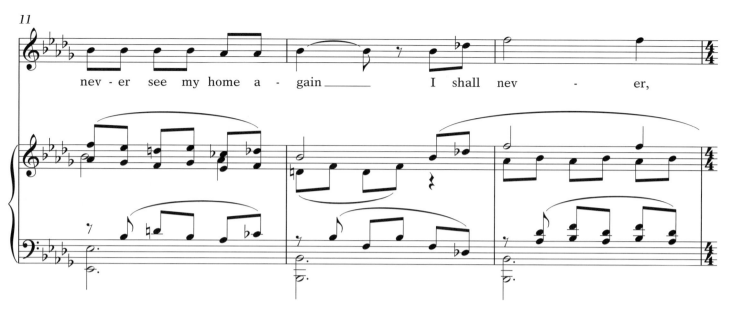

nev-er see my home a - gain _____ I shall nev - er,

nev-er see my home a - gain. _____

Andante agitato

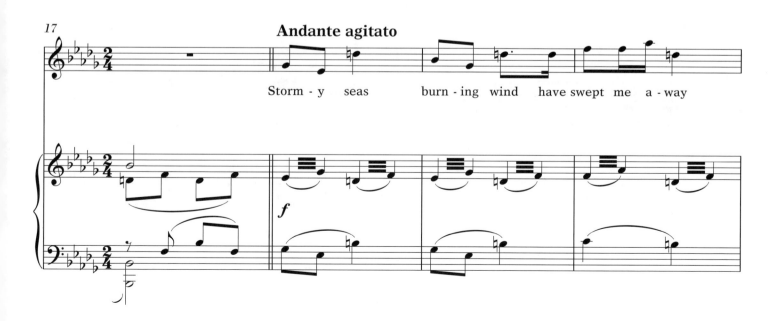

Storm - y seas burn - ing wind have swept me a - way

swept me a-way. With cries of fear and joy___ I let my

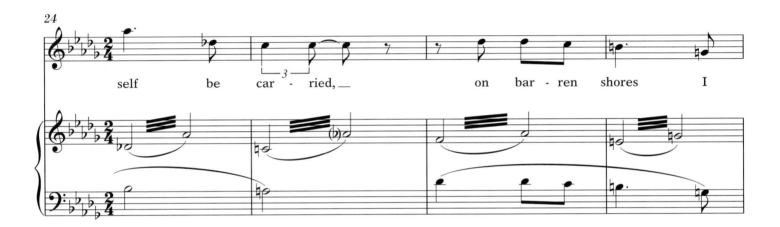

self be car - ried, ___ on bar - ren shores I

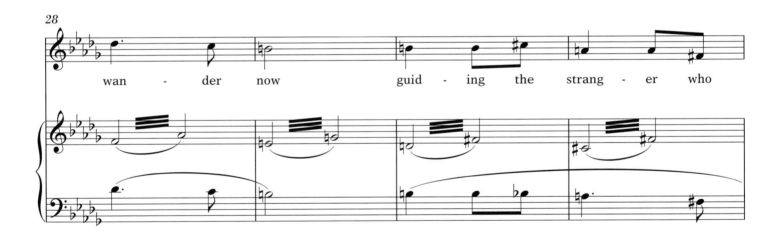

wan - der now guid - ing the strang - er who

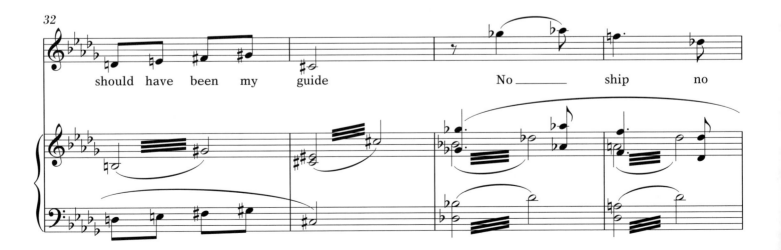

should have been my guide No ___ ship no

light to show the way; no hope for back - ward

jour - ney. The chil - dren's isle is_____ for - ev - er

lost for - ev - er for - ev - er lost

sempre più rall.

Tempo I

Oh how

far how far my bed-room sky how far my wind tor-ment-ed

cy - press tree. Oh where_____ my moth-er's scent - ed room?

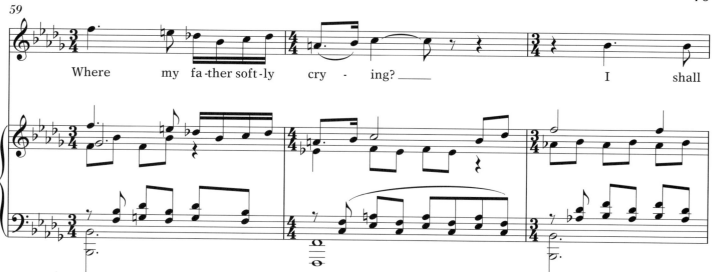

Where my fa-ther soft-ly cry - ing? _____ I shall

nev - er see my home a - gain, I shall nev - er

rall. **a tempo**

nev - er see my home a - gain. _____